Know

what I know?

The Symbols of Christmas

Do Open before Christmas

Created and Compiled by
Jim Cook

Edited by
Shannon Gridley

Cover Art by
Doug Howard

Do You Know What I Know?
Box 141184
Orlando, FL 32814
Voice 407-645-2665 Fax 407-645-2665

ISBN: 0-929987-26-8

Printed in the United States of America

TABLE OF CONTENTS

INTRODUCTION

Every generation has contributed to the vast store of American Christmas lore. From the rites of ancient man...To the mid-winter festivals...To the modern Christmas! Many customs, symbols, dates and traditions have so crisscrossed, intertwined and entangled themselves, they have lost their original significance to the people who celebrate Christmas.

For instance... Did you know that:

- Jesus was likely born in August or September in 3-4 B.C? (Look under *Herod*.)
- December 25, now Christmas Day, was an arbitrary date selected to superimpose itself on a pagan holiday? (See *December 25*.)

We hope *Do You Know What I Know ?* is informative for all who read it, for those who do not understand the elements behind the Christmas lore, and that the whole family may understand "the myths behind the myths." Plus!... Some *secret* recipes of the season.

DEDICATION

To Doug Howard for great cover art and, especially, to Shannon Gridley, the editor of this project.

To the immediate family of Ashleigh, Dave, J J, Judy, and, especially, Janice. Thank you all for putting up with my "personality" quirks during the research and compilation of this book.

To the extended family of Tiffany, Maria and Lisa for reasons you will not understand, I thank you.

As in any project, there always seems to be one person who is on your mind when trying to start and finish any lengthy endeavor. Someone who supplies that sense of urgency to achieve a final result, and I will never be able to thank her. Rainbow, wherever you are: BE HAPPY!

And, finally, to my readers: I hope you enjoy *Do You Know What I Know?*. If there is some symbol you believe should be added to the next edition, please fill out the form below and send to:

>Jim Cook
>Box 4814
>Winter Park, FL 32793

List below any customs, symbols, etc., that you feel were omitted from this edition. (Use additional pages if necessary.)

_____

_____

A

Aaaaah! - What children exclaim when they glimpse their first fully
decorated Christmas Tree.

A.D. - *ANNO DOMINI* - In The Year of Our Lord - The beginning of modern
Christian system of dating.

Advent - A period of time to prepare for Christ's birth, His Coming. The Advent
practice began in the 6th century. It begins the 1st Sunday nearest the
Feast of St. Andrew, which is November 30 and embraces the four
consecutive Sundays before the Christmas Day. The word itself derived
from the Latin *adventus* meaning "to come."

Advent Calendar - Begins on Advent Sunday and ends Christmas Day.
Some calendars have windows that are "opened" daily and these
windows contain pictures related to the Christmas Story.

Advent Candles (three purple and one pink) - One lit on each Sunday until all
candles are lit by the Sunday before Christmas Day.

Advent Sunday - The first Sunday in Advent.

Advent Wreath - Originally from Germany. Though American wreaths are
traditionally circular, the German advent wreath is usually a horizontal
evergreen, decorated with gold, purple and red ribbons. Either wreath
should contain the four Advent Candles (three purple, one pink).
See *Wreath*.

Alleluia - Hebrew term meaning *Praise Ye Yah*. Hebrew tradition does not allow
the name of God spoken by man. *Yah,* an abbreviation of *Yah Weh*
meaning "God with no name."

Angels - Bodiless, immortal spirits that appear to mankind at important
moments. The angels appear to man as messengers of God, bringing
messages of comfort, warnings, tests of belief, and deliverance. They
are also bringers of peace and goodwill. The New Testament tells how
the *Angel of the Lord* appeared to the *shepherds keeping watch over
their flocks* to bring them *good tidings of great joy* - The Birth of Christ.
And the multitude of angels proclaimed:

> *Glory to God in the Highest*
> *and on earth, peace,*
> *goodwill toward men.*

Animals - Animals are constantly alluded to in the Christmas Pageants. Here are a few of their tales. (Also refer to *(The) Friendly Beast Song*, a humorous poem of the animals interaction on Christmas Eve.)

Bees-hummed a Christmas Carol.

Beetle-because of its size, it was only noticed by Jesus. When touched it became a glow-worm, its light to guide travelers.

Cat-appeared, but disdained to join the kneeling beasts and only mumbled in recognition. Amused at its independence, Mary blessed it, saying that it would always live at man's hearth but never be man's servant.

Camels-have long represented religious traditions.

Cow-donated his fresh hay to Mary for the Baby's bed, and warmed the Child with his breath.

Doves-cooed Jesus to sleep.

Nightingale-this bird had never sung before that night, but the choir of angels roused it and the bird caroled with them.

Owl-did not rouse itself to join its fellow animals, and was condemned to perpetual penance, hiding by day and by night crying "Who will guide me to the new born? Who? Who?"

Robin-fanned the fire in the cave at Bethlehem and kept it burning throughout the night. It's red breast, singed by the flames, became its mark of generosity.

Rooster-crowed all night.

Sheep--gave Mary the wool to weave a soft blanket.

Stork-plucked its own feathers to soften the Infant's bed and so remained the patron of babies ever after.

All farm animals show their adoration on Christmas Eve by falling on their knee's at midnight. Certain animals are given the gift of speech for one hour to announce the Birth of Christ, but it is bad luck for humans who hear those words.

Apple(s) - It was a magical fruit to the ancients. Its juices fermented into a liquor, its fruit outlived other fruits, thus the apple gave food and cheer at the time when, in the depths of winter, man had neither. The apple also represented man's fall from Paradise, as the forbidden fruit of Eden.

𝕭

Bah! Humbug! - Bah! from French *Bah!* (a term exclaiming scorn) and *Humbug!* from Mid-18th century English slang word for *trick*, sham or nonsense; a *hoax!*

Balthasar - One of the Three Wise Men. King of Sheba or Ethiopia or Chaldea. He was tall, dark skinned, bearded, 40 years of age and his gift to Christ was Frankincense, a token of divinity and which depicts the death of the Son of man. See *Magi* and *Three Kings.*

Banning of Christmas - A period from 1644 to 1656 when Christmas was not celebrated in England or America. See *No Christmas* and *Puritans.*

Bay (leaf) - From the laurel bush, it was the first plant used to honor Christ's Birthday.

B.C. - Before the Common Era or Before Christ.

Bells - The first bells came from China, but all ancient religions and societies used them for their ceremonies. Bells evolved from the rattles of savages into the sweet-toned silver bells. Though the church did not use bells until the 6th century, in Medieval Europe they were used to warn the devil of the coming birth of the Christ who would save the world from darkness and sin.
The bells used by Santa's "helpers" for charity came from the Middle Ages when the poor rang hand bells for alms.

Bertha/Hertha/Freke/Perchta - From Northern European customs, this goddess's contribution to the modern Christmas tradition is the coming down the chimney. To the ancients she would descend into the dining area during the celebration of the winter solstice, coming through the smoke of the hearth, bringing happiness and goodwill.

Bible - The word Bible is derived from the Greek *bibila* meaning "books," and refers to the sacred writings of both Judaism and Christianity. The bible consists of two parts, called the Old Testament (First five books are called the TORAH (law) in Judaism). The second part, called the New Testament, was composed in Greek (*See Septuagint*) and records the story of Jesus and the beginnings of Christianity.

Birth (of Christ) - Early Christians did not celebrate the birth of Christ, but rather celebrated his Resurrection as celebrating anyone's birthday was considered a pagan custom. The Bible gives no clues as to His birth date, so to the early Christians, this modern festival was not even an event of note. As times and perspectives changed, a more historical determination was sought. Hippolytis (236 A.D.) calculated Christ must have been born on a Wednesday, the same day God created the sun. For others, the first day of creation coincided with the first day of spring, March 21, and it was contended that Jesus's birthday fell four days later, on March 24. Others maintained that May 20, April 19, and April 20 were His Birthdates. See *December 25* and *Christmas Day*.

Big Book (Santa's) - THE book in which Santa would keep the records of the children's behavior. See *Black Peter* and *Nast, Thomas*.

Birthdays on Christmas:

Clara Barton - Founder of American Red Cross
Humphrey Bogart - Actor
Jimmy Buffet - Singer
Cab Calloway - Band Leader
Robin Campbell - Reggae singer
Louis Chevrolet - Car Manufacturer
Alice Cooper - Singer
Larry Csonka - Football player
Conrad Hilton - Hotelier
Lord Grade - Producer
Noel Hogan - Rock musician
Howard Hughes - Businessman
Robert Joffrey - Joffrey Ballet
Annie Lennox - Singer
Barbara Mandrell - Singer
Tony Martin - Singer
Shane McGowan - Singer
Sir Isaac Newton - Physicist
Kid Ory - New Orleans Jazz Musician
Little Richard (Richard Penniman) - Rock and Roll Singer
Robert Ripley - *Ripley's Believe it or Not!*
Anwar Sadat - Statesman and Prime Minister of Egypt
Gary Sandy - Actor
Rod Serling - TV Producer
Sissy Spacek - Actress
Ken Stabler - Football player
Lisa Bell Acheson Wallace - co-founder of *Reader's Digest*
Steve Warner - Country Singer

Black Peter - St. Nicholas' servant and companion from the Netherlands. He would keep the records of children's behavior in a big book. Where St. Nicholas would give sweets and presents, Black Pete would be the giver of lumps of coal to bad little boys and girls. This legend comes from the Spanish Moors who were black African conquerors of the Iberian Peninsula.

Boars Head - Seen in the art of the mid -18th century, served on a silver tray with an apple in it's mouth! Originally a Scandinavian Yule tradition, the wild boar was sacrificed to Thea - The Goddess of love and fertility. As time evolved and the wild boar disappeared, it was replaced by the Christmas Pig. Now all that is left of this ancient tradition is the Christmas Ham.

Boxing Day - December 26 or St. Stephen's Day. As Christmas Day was a very generous day for the church "poor box," this alms box would be broken and distributed on the day after Christmas. So Boxing Day has nothing to do with gift boxes, but the "poor box." In Holland, children would save pennies for the poor in pig-shaped earthenware boxes. Originally called "feast pig" (now called piggy banks) and the monies saved were distributed on the day after Christmas.

℃

Caesar Augustus - Roman ruler who set in motion the Christmas Holidays. He decreed that all men must be counted in a census and taxed. All peoples must go to the birth city of the head male of the family. Joseph was born in Bethlehem, City of David, so Mary and Joseph were sent to Bethlehem, where Christ was born.

Candle(s) - The ancient world had been using candles since 3000 B.C. and the ceremonies using candles go back into the mist of time. The ancients used them to prolong the day and scare away the terrors of darkness, to defy the Frost King. Candles became a symbol of enlightenment, expressing joy. The Romans exchanged glowing tapers as expressions of goodwill and affection during Saturnalia. The Jews had their Feast of Lights. See *Hanukkah*.
The use of candles for the Christmas celebration was absorbed into the symbol of Jesus as the Light of the World, a symbol of everlasting life. Candlelight became a symbol of the banishment of the darkness of paganism. Candles in paper bags are called luminaries.

Candles in the Window - This tradition comes from the Irish. When Christianity was suppressed in Ireland, the priest had to travel through the night. Irish Christians left their doors unlocked and candles in the windows to show welcome to the priests and to guide them through the dark night. When the English authorities questioned them, they simply explained that the candles were for Mary and Joseph.

Candy Canes - Represent the shepherd's crook. The source for the striped pattern has two legends:
- Patterned after the barber pole
- Pure white for the Virgin Birth; "J" to represent the name of Jesus and his staff; red stripes- three small to show scouring of Jesus, one large stripe for the blood shed by Christ.

Cards - This very modern tradition evolved from English school boys in the early 1800's. They would send 'Christmas pieces' or greetings to their parents. They were written on decorated sheets to show off their progress in composition and penmanship. In 1842, a William Egley tried to make a commercial success of Christmas cards but failed to arouse any interest. In 1847, Sir Henry Cole commissioned J.C. Horsely to make a card. There was little interest at first, but by 1868, it was a common practice in all of England. Louis Prange began the public sale of Christmas cards in America in 1875.

Carols - Comes from the Greek word: *oraulein* - choros - "the dance," and *aulein* - "play the flute."
- The original meaning of the word carol, was a circular dance with no songs, simply to dance in a circle listening to a flute.
  By the Middle Ages it became *carollen* - "to sing joyfully" - when troupes of costumed actors traveled from village to village presenting the Christmas plays in song. The earliest dated carol was in 129 A.D.
- Carols are very secular, joyous songs, sung in the common tongue, versus hymns which are very solemn and sung in High Latin.
- The Father of the Christmas Carol is attributed to St. Francis, the originator of Nativity scenes, who taught his people to "tell of your Christmas joy in songs."

Caspar/Gasper - One of The Three Wise Men. He was the King of Tarus. He was short, of ruddy hue, beardless, 20 years of age and his gift to Christ was Myrrh, a token of truth and meekness and homage due to Divinity.

Cherry (tree) - The ancients would take a sprig off the cherry tree and force it to flower at the winter solstice, an omen of good luck.
- A Christmas legend: Once Joseph became betrothed to Mary and found she was with child, he felt disgraced. As with any pregnant woman, Mary had cravings, one of which was to eat cherries. She asked Joseph to pluck some for her, but angered and filled with suspicion and reproach, he refused. He said "Let the father of the baby gather the cherries" and, at once, a voice sang a command, and a cherry tree bent its branches so that the fruit fell into her lap.

Chimney - See *Bertha* and *St. Nicholas*.

Christ - From Greek word *khristos* meaning "Messiah"; *khristos* from *Chi-rho* signifying a symbol of Messiah.

Christmas - Meaning the Mass of Christ. The word itself comes from *Christ* and the Olde English word *masesse* meaning "feast"- Feast of Christ.

A Christmas Carol - Charles Dickens classic Christmas tale written in 1843. Its main characters were Scrooge and Tiny Tim.

Christmas Day - The traditional day for the celebration of Christ's Birth. Though it is the considered opinion of many that this is not his date of birth, it was officially declared Christ Day of Birth by Pope Julius I around 350 A.D. This date was picked, not from evidence, but for many and varied reasons.
- One explanation centers around the ancient winter festivals of early man that had been around thousands of years before Christianity. These festivals were based on the Winter Solstice, the shortest day of the year. These primitive societies connected these midwinter festivals with the fertility of the earth, with the Winter Solstice being the ONE festival needed to rescue the sun from total disappearance. This was a universal date, December 21, the shortest day of the year in all parts of the world. This date was feared and celebrated by all cultures and ancient man would not give up this important event.
- Another explanation comes to us from our ancient history. Around the same time Christianity was beginning, another rival religion became the official religion of the State of Rome. Myrtharism was devoted to the goddess of the Unconquered Sun, Mythra. Its major holiday was December 25, to celebrate the birth of this goddess. The early Christian priests could not get everyone to forget their old gods and pagan holidays so the priests simply placed Christian holidays on the same days of the year. They wanted Christian holidays to slowly replace the pagan ones, so the rebirth of the Unconquered Sun became the Birth of the Son.
See *Birth of Christ* and *December 25*.

Christmas Rose/White Christmas Rose - To ease the heart of Maiden Madeline, the sister of Mary, who arrived empty handed at Bethlehem, the Arch Angel Gabriel struck the ground and caused the Christmas Rose to bloom.

City of David - The same as Bethlehem, city of King David, and Joseph's and Jesus' place of birth.

Colly Bird - from the *Twelve Days of Christmas* Song. Lyric incorrectly pronounced "calling bird." Colly originally meant "black" or "black bird," which was a staple food source in this era.

Colors • Red: fire, blood, warmth, Santa's cloak, Charity, excitement.
      • White: crisp frosty snow, light of the stars, candles, Santa's
                  beard, angels' robes, church color for purity.
      • Green: symbol of nature, evergreens, Christmas trees glistening,
                  banners of vitality, breath of health, youth and eternal life.
      • Gold: sunlight, angels' halos, shining tinsel, radiance.
      • Silver: "reflects" the entire season.

Cookies - From Dutch word *koek* meaning "cake." See *Food.*

Crackers (not a food item) - a bag of goodies enclosed in a paper covering.
      When tugged hard, they burst open to release the contents. Invented
      in England in 1860 by John Smith.

Crib/Cre'che/Cradle - Nativity scene introduced by St. Francis of Assisi in
      1223 A.D., as a means to instruct the poor, uneducated masses
      about the Glory of the Christmas Holiday; a somewhat miniature
      Bethlehem stable.

Crosby, Bing - American Singer who sang the most popular Christmas
      song/carol, *White Christmas*, in the movie *Holiday Inn*.

Currency - Santa Claus once pictured on legal currency. Before the Civil War,
      Santa was used on bank-issued currency, including three-dollar bills.

                                    𝔇

Daisy - Christmas Legend: a shepherd boy was left to attend the fires as the
      grown-up shepherds went to visit the Christ Child. The little shepherd
      boy decided to go, but had no gifts to offer. He remembered a flower
      he had seen on the way and offered it to Christ. Christ grasped the
      flower and raised it to his lips, touched it and the beautiful golden
      color appeared.

Dashing (through the snow) - comes from Middle English *daschen*
      meaning "to strike," as in to strike a whip.

Deaths on Christmas Day:
          Johnny Ace - Singer
          Joan Blondell - Actress
          Samuel de Champlain - Explorer
          Charlie Chaplin - Entertainer
          W.C. Fields - Comedian
          Billy Martin - Baseball
          Dean Martin - Entertainer
          Nick the Greek - Gambler

December - Originates from Latin *decem* meaning ten. In the Olde Roman calendar, December was the 10th month, with March being the beginning of the Roman year. King Pompilis added January and February as a means of 'modernizing' the dating system, but December remained the last month of the year.

December 25 - There is no reason to believe Jesus was born on this date. Neither Matthew or Luke provide any indications of His birth date. Dionysius Exiguus introduced the Christian calendar, but miscalculated by several years the true date of birth. Historical research indicates Herod died in 1 B.C. Herod's edict that all male children 2 years and younger be slaughtered in an attempt to destroy Jesus, but history shows Christ escaped to Egypt in 2-3 B.C., so Christ was alive at this time (2-3 B.C.), the approximate year of his true birth. Further, since the winters are very cold in Palestine, and the shepherds would not have been in the fields at night, the assumption is that he was born either in August or September. Astronomically, the year 2-3 B.C. coordinates with a triple conjunction of Jupiter (Kings Planet), Venus (Mother Planet) and Regulus (King Star) in the late summer, which could be construed as the Star of Bethlehem.
See *Birth of Christ* and *Christmas Day.*

Deck (the halls) - This word comes from Middle Dutch *deken* meaning "to cover"; later it took on the meaning "to clothe in specially beautiful or ornamental attire."

Dickens, Charles - Famous English author who wrote *A Christmas Carol* in 1843.

Dionysius - Conceived the idea of introducing a Christian calendar. He based the date of birth on the founding of Rome in 754 B.C. He inaccurately assigned the year 1 A.D. on this assumption, a mistake of four years.

Druids - An ancient pagan cult that lived in England and Northern Europe. They worshipped gods of nature, believed in reincarnation and immortality. Some of their religious rites involved oak trees that held the mistletoe that has become part of our Christmas.

Eden Tree - Part of the Paradise or Miracle Plays that were used to show unsophisticated peasants the pageantry of Christmas. Legend has it that Adam and Eve brought a twig of The Tree of Hidden Fruit out of Eden and that it became the wood of the Holy Cross.

Egg Nog - The original Egg Nog was a strong beer with eggs beaten until foamy. Then cider, wines and hard liquor were substituted for beer. 'Egg 'n grog' was the original combination of eggs, milk, sugar and spiced rum (grog).

Egg Nog - George Washington's Recipe:

1 quart milk　　　　　　　*1 pint brandy*
1 quart cream　　　　　　*1/2 pint rye whiskey*
1 dozen eggs　　　　　　*1/4 pint Dark rum*
1 dozen tablespoons　　　*1/4 pint sherry*
sugar

Mix liquor first. Separate yolks and whites of eggs. Add sugar to beaten yolks, gradually add milk. Mix well. Add liquor mixture, drop by drop at first, slowly beating. Beat whites of eggs until stiff and fold slowly into mixture. Let it sit in refrigerator for several days. Serve topped with whipped cream. Yields 3 1/2 quarts.

Electric lights/bulbs - In 1895, as the candles on drying trees would cause fires, Ralph Morris of New England Telephone and Telegraph fashioned strings of lights from telephone switchboard bulbs.

Elves (Santa's) - Santa's helpers grew from the Scandinavian trolls or *Julenisse* (which also was the root of Leprechaun legends). They began appearing in modern Christmas myths around the mid-1850's. See *Gnomes.*

Emmanuel (Immanuel) - Hebrew for "God is with us." It also means an appearance of God or any other supernatural being.

England - The great traditions of Christmas for America and England are so intertwined that there is little difference between England's Father Christmas and America's Santa Claus. Most of the other shared traditions of our great feast were initiated from England.

Entertainment: (Live and animated movies) -

Adventure: *Miracle Down Under*
Santa Claus: The Movie

Children: *Babar and Father Christmas*
The Bear Who slept Through Christmas
The Berenstain Bear's Christmas Tree
A Charlie Brown Christmas
A Charlie Brown Christmas, You're Not Elected
Christmas Eve On Sesame Street
Christmas Stories
Disney Christmas Gifts
The First Christmas
Frosty the Snowman
How the Flintstones Saved Christmas
How the Grinch Stole Christmas
Jack Frost
The Jetson's Christmas Carol
Jiminy Cricket's Christmas
The Little Drummer Boy
Madeline's Christmas
Mickey's Christmas Carol
Mister Magoo's Christmas Carol
Nestor, The Long-Eared Christmas Donkey
The Night Before Christmas
Santa Bear's High Flying Christmas
Santa Bear's First Christmas
Snowman
The Tailor of Glouster
Trolls and The Christmas Express
Twas the Night Before Christmas
A Very Merry Cricket
Why Christmas Trees Aren't Perfect
Winnie the Pooh and Christmas, Too
Yes! Virginia, there is a Santa Claus

Comedy: *Bishop's Wife*
Christmas In Connecticut
Christmas in July
Home Alone
Home Alone 2: Lost in New York
Jingle All the Way
Miracle on 34th Street
Scrooged
Pocketful of Miracles
National Lampoon's Christmas Vacation

Entertainment - (continued) -

Drama: *An American Christmas Carol*
Christmas Carol (1933, 1938, 1951)
Homecoming
It's a Wonderful Life
Man in the Santa Claus Suit
Nightmare Before Christmas
Year without Santa Claus

Family: *Babes in Toyland*
Babysitters Club: Special Christmas
Captain Kangaroo's Merry Christmas
Child's Christmas in Wales
Christmas Story
The Christmas That Almost Wasn't
McGee and Me: Twas the Flight Before Christmas
The Muppet Christmas Carol
The Night They Saved Christmas
One Magic Christmas
Prancer
Rudolph the Red-Nosed Reindeer
Santa Claus is Coming to Town
Spirit of the Season
Waltons: The Christmas Carol
Year Without Santa Claus

Musical: *Holiday Inn*
Meet Me in St. Louis
Scrooge
White Christmas

Religion: *Greatest Adventure of the Nativity*
Nativity

Epiphany - Greek word for *manifestation*. This feast is celebrated on January 6 or the 12th night of Christmas, which coincides with the coming of the Magi to Bethlehem. This date was also associated with a major pagan festival associated with rivers and the water gods. The Church replaced this pagan celebration early in the 4th century by commemorating the baptism of Christ in the Jordan River by John the Baptist. It became Christ's spiritual birthday.

Evergreens - Represents all the plants that withstood the death of winter and so were charged with enchanted powers which signified the strength of life. These evergreens were symbols of eternal life and thought to bring good luck against evil spirits. The ancients held the evergreens as protectors and brought them inside to keep the evil of darkness at bay. After all, the plants were man's hope that the sun would return. From two Olde English terms: *"aefre"* meaning "always."
: *"growan"* meaning "to grow."

ℱ

ℱather Christmas - The English equivalent of the American Santa Claus. Tall stately gift-bringer with a long white beard. Wears a green robe with holly/ivy wreath hood. Originally not a gift-giver, but the soul of winter, serving as a master of ceremonies.

Festivals - Periods for merrymaking or celebrations. Once considered a day of feasting and celebration related to the rhythm of the seasons and, now, the mysteries of faith when related to the Modern Christmas.

Fir Tree - Important evergreen for the holiday. To the ancients, it represented the spirits of fertility. From time immemorial, people would bring into their hovel these symbols of everlasting life. Legend has it that when Eve plucked the fruit of the Tree of Life that grew in Eden, its flowers shrank into needles.

Fire - It was the center of all winter festivals, brother to the sun and the "calling out to the heavens." To the ancients, fire meant safety and security from wild beasts and evil, dark spirits.

Food (cookies and milk) - The tradition of milk and cookies left out for Santa came from the ancient rites of leaving food out for gods, ghosts and goblins that walked the earth during winter's longest night - the winter solstice.

Frankincense - Gift to Christ from Caspar, one of the Three Wise Men. A rare and sacred resin that was the symbol of divinity and of a high priest; a sweet spice representing prayer and also homage due a King of Heaven. Pragmatically, used to ward off stable smells.

(The) Friendly Beasts song:

Jesus, our brother, kind and good
Was humbly born in a stable rude.
The friendly beasts around Him stood
Jesus, our brother, kind and good.

I, said the donkey, all shaggy and brown
I carried His mother uphill and down.
I carried her safely to Bethle'm town
I, said the donkey, all shaggy and brown.

I, said the cow all white and red
I gave Him my manger for a bed.
I gave Him my hay to pillow his head
I, said the cow, all white and red.

I, said the sheep with the curly horn
I gave Him my wool for a blanket warm.
He wore my coat on Christmas morn
I, said the sheep with the curly horn.

I, said the dove from the rafter high
I cooed Him to sleep so He would not cry.
We cooed Him to sleep my mate and I
I, said the dove from the rafter high.

So every beast, by some good spell
In the stable rude was glad to tell
Of the gift he gave Emmanuel,
The gift he gave Emmanuel.

See *Animals*.

Fruitcake - Originally an English dessert for the Feast of the Epiphany or 12th day of Christmas. Some people insist that one of the original cakes from the Mid-18th century is still being given at Christmas.

Fruitcake recipe - (a delicious version)

1 cup sugar
1/2 pound butter
5 large eggs
1 3/4 cups flour
1/2 teaspoon baking powder
1/2 ounce lemon extract
1/2 ounce vanilla extact

3/4 pound candied cherries, chopped
1 pound candied pineapple, chopped
4 cups pecans, chopped
1/4 pound whole candied cherries
1/4 pound candied pineapple slices
30-40 pecans

Grease angel food cake pan or 5 loaf pans (or spray with non-stick spray). In large bowl of electric mixer, blend sugar and butter thoroughly. Add eggs one at a time until well mixed. Add flour and baking powder and continue beating. Add extracts when batter well-blended and smooth. Stir in chopped cherries, pineapple and pecans, mixing well to distribute evenly. Pour in pan and decorate with whole cherries, pineapple slices (which have been sliced once and halved), and pecan halves. Bake in cold oven at 250 degrees for 3 hours. Cool thoroughly, remove from pan, wrap and store in cool, dark place until ready to serve.
Yield: one 5-pound cake or five 1-pound cakes.

Garland - Garlands are swags or hanging sprays of evergreen branches, wired together and hung inside the house as decorations. The ancient Druids believed that to bring evergreens into the home would bring good luck and this tradition is still with us today.

Gaspar (Casper) - See *Caspar.*

Gifts - The ancients used gifts for goodwill and magic during the season of the returning sun. Our modern tradition of gifts began with the Roman mid-winter festival Saturnalia, where they would offer gifts to their poor neighbors. The church simply transferred its significance to a ritual commemorating the gifts of the Magi. We place them under the tree, whereas the early German tradition had gifts being attached to the tree limbs. As the gifts got larger they eventually had to be placed under it rather than in it.
See *Saturnalia.*

Gifts of the Magi - See *Regal Gifts of the Magi.*

Gift-givers - Gift-givers have been with mankind since well before the ancients. It has always been mankind's desire to share and the gift-givers came out of this yearning. These gift-givers or gift-bearers have evolved from local customs and traditions and have grown over the centuries. A small listing by country:

Austria-Krampus	Italy-Befana
Belgium-Saint Nicholas	Japan-Hoteiosho
Brazil-Papa Noel	Korea-Santa Claus
Bulgaria-Grandfather Koleda	Lebanon-Magic Mule
China-Dun lao ren	Mexico-The Three Wise Men
Chile-Viejo Pascuero	Norway-Julenisse
Costa Rica-Christ Child	Poland-Star Man
England-Father Christmas	Russia-Babouschka
Finland-Father Christmas	Spain-The Three Wise Men
France-Pere Noel	Sweden-Jultomte
Germany-Khristkindle	Switzerland-Samichulas
Guatemala-Christ Child	Syria-The Smallest Camel
Holland-Sinter Klaas	United States-Santa Claus
Hungary-Mikulas	Wales-Father Christmas

Gingerbread - These are shaped cookies and cakes from the 15th century. They were edible figurines (dolls) that substituted for the human sacrifices of the ancients.

Gingerbread Boys/Girls recipe -

1 cup shortening	*1 1/2 teaspoons soda*
1 cup granulated sugar	*1/2 teaspoon salt*
1 egg	*2 to 3 teaspoons ginger*
1 cup molasses	*1 teaspoon cinnamon*
2 tablespoons vinegar	*1 teaspoon cloves*
5 cups sifted all-purpose flour	*cinnamon candies*

Thoroughly cream shortening with sugar. Stir in egg, molasses, and vinegar; beat well. Sift together dry ingredients; stir in molasses mixture, mixing well. Chill at least 3 hours.
On lightly floured surface, roll dough to 1/8 inch thickness. Cut with appropriate shaped cookie cutter. Place 1 inch apart on greased cookie sheet. Use red cinnamon candies for faces and buttons. Bake at 375 degrees for 5 to 6 minutes. Cool slightly; remove from sheet and cool. Note: for an even richer recipe use brewed coffee instead of water. Makes 5 dozen 4-inch cookies. Gingerbread house represents the home, a symbol of security and warmth.

Gnomes - (Santa's Helpers) Were miniature Father Christmases called *nisse* from Norway and Sweden legends. A dwarf that dwells in the earth and guards its treasures; also the basic legend for leprechauns.

Gold - Gift to Christ from Melchior, one of the Three Wise Men. A precious metal that was the symbol of the power of Kings and light. As a pragmatic matter, gold was intended to ease Mary's poverty.

The Gospel according to St. Luke: Chapter II: 1-20

> *And it came to passe in those dayes, that there went out a decree from Cesar Augustus, that all the world should be taxed.*
>
> *2 (And this taxing was first made when Cyrenius was governor of Syria)*
>
> *3 And all went to be taxed, every one into his owne citie.*
>
> *4 And Joseph also went up from Galilee, out of the citie of Nazareth, into Judea, unto the citie of David, which is called Bethlehem, (because he was of the house and linage of David)*
>
> *5 To be taxed with Mary his espoused wife, being great with child.*
>
> *6 And so it was, that while they were there, the dayes were a accomplished that she should deliver.*
>
> *7 And she brought forth her first borne sonne, and wrapped him in swaddling clothes, and laid him in a manger, because there was no roome for them in the Inne.*
>
> *8 And there were in the same countrey, shepheards abiding in ye field, keeping watch over their flocke by night.*
>
> *9 And loe, the Angel of the Lord came upon them, and the glory of the Lord shone round them, and they were sore afraid.*
>
> *10 And the Angel said unto them, Feare not: For behold, I bring you good tidings of great joy, which shall be to all people.*
>
> *11 For unto you is borne this day, in the citie of David, a Saviour which is Christ the Lord.*
>
> *12 And this shall be a signe unto you; yee shall find the babe wrapped in swaddling clothes lying in a manger.*
>
> *13 And suddenly there was with the Angel a multitude of the heavenly hoste praising God and saying,*

14 Glory to God in the highest, and on earth peace, good will towards men.

15 And it came to passe, as the Angels were gone away from them into heaven, the shepheards said one to another, Let us now goe even unto Bethlehem, and see this which is come to passe, which the Lord hath made knowen unto us.

16 And they came with haste, and found Mary and Joseph, and the babe lying in a manger.

17 And when they had seene it, they made knowen abroad the saying, which was told them, concerning this child.

18 And all they that heard it, wondered at those things, which were tolde them by the shepheards.

19 But Mary kept all these things, and pondered them in her heart.

20 And the shepheards returned, glorifying and praising God for all the things that they had heard and, as it was told unto them.

The Gospel According to St. Matthew: Chapter II: 1-12

Now when Jesus was borne in Bethlehem of Judea, in the dayes of Herod the king, behold, there came Wise men from the East to Jierusalem,

2 Saying, Where is he that is borne King of the Jewes: for we have scene his Starre in the East, and are come to worship him.

3 When Herod the king had heard these things, he was troubled, and all Jierusalem with him.

4 And when he had gathered all the chiefe Priests and Scribes of the people together, hee demanded of them where Christ should be borne.

5 And they said unto him, In Bethlehem of Judea: for thus it is written by the Prophet;

6 And thou Bethlehem in the land of Judea, art not the least among the Princes of Juda: for out of thee shall come a Governour, that shall rule my people Israel.

7 Then Herod, when he had privily called the Wise men, enquired of them diligently what time this Starre appeared:

8 And he sent them to Bethlehem, and said, Goe, and search diligently for the yong child, and when ye have found him, bring me word againe, that I may come and worship him also.

9 When they had heard the king, they departed, and loe, the Starre which they saw in the East, went before them, till it came and stood over where the younge child was.

10 When they saw the Starre, they reioyced with exceeding great ioy.

11 And when they were come into the house, they saw the yong child with Mary his mother, and fell downe, and worshiped him: and when they had opened their treasures, they presented unto him gifts, gold, frankincense, and myrrhe.

12 And being warned by God in a dreame, that they should not returne to Herod, they departed into their owne countrey another way.

Greetings - *"Merry Christmas"* in other countries:

China-*Sheng Dan Jieh*
Denmark-*Glaedelig Jul*
England-*Happy Christmas*
Finland-*Hauskaa Joulua*
France-*Joyeux Noel*
Germany-*Froehliche Weihnachten*
Greece-*Efihismena Christougenna*
Holland-*Zalig Kerstfeest*
Italy-*Buon Natale*
Japan-*Meri Kurisumasu*
Mexico-*Feliz Navidad*
Norway-*Gledelig Jul*
Poland-*Wesolych Swait*
Portugal-*Boas Festas*
Romania-*Sarbatori Vesele*
Russia-*Hristos Razdajetsja*
Spain-*Felices Pascuas*
Sweden-*Glad Jul*
Wales-*Nadolog Llawen*

H

Ham - Christmas Ham! Remnant of the Scandinavian tradition of feasting where the Wild Boar was the main course. As the Wild Boar died out, tradition substituted domestic pig for the main course, now the modern Christmas celebration uses a simple ham.

Hanukkah (Chanukah) - Jewish Festival of Lights. This Feast of Lights was another midwinter festival that cross-referenced into the December 25 date selection by the Christian Church. This feast celebrates the victory of Judah McCabee over the Syrians. It celebrates the miracle of eternal light where the Jews had oil for only one night, but it lasted a full seven nights to break the siege.

Herbs - Besides their use in cooking, herbs accented the holiday scents. Early use was to spread branches, twigs, leaves etc. on the floor and, when dancing took place they perfumed the air.

Herald Angels - An Angel that delivers news. Note: In the United States a number of newspapers still title themselves with the name *Herald* because it means a person who announces significant news.

Herod - A brutal ruler who governed Palestine during the rule of Caesar Augustus. As a puppet king, he was loyal to neither Rome or the Jews. Though his recorded death was in 1 B.C., he fell from power in 3-4 B.C. (Another point of historial fact and fiction not agreeing - e.g. Christ's birth supposedly 0 A.D., yet Christ was born when Herod was alive 1 to 4 B.C.) When learning of a "King of the Jews" being born in Bethlehem, Herod ordered the massacre of all the infants in the City of David. God warned Joseph in a dream of the coming slaughter, and Joseph took Mary and Jesus to Egypt.

Hessians - German mercenaries during the American Revolution, sometimes credited with introducing the Christmas tree to America. (Remember history, when George Washington crossed the Delaware River on Christmas Day to defeat the Hessians.)

Hobby Horse - The traditional Christmas present is a descendant of the Viking midwinter feast, Yule (Jul), when the early Norsemen would use a live animal as a sacrifice to the All-Father Odin as part of the celebration and offering.

Holiday - A day set aside for holy worship. It was written *halliday* or "holy day" until the 16th century when the term went from religious days to also include any day devoted to recreation and not work. Variation from Olde English *halig* meaning "hold" and *doed* meaning "day."

Holly - From Olde English *holegn* or *holen*. This plant was believed magical by the ancient Druids because it retained its leaves and bore fruit well into winter. It was thought to be mystical because the Druids believed the fairies and gnomes who lived in the holly trees came indoors in winter to allow their spirits to escape the hardships outside.
  • Considered the Thorn of Crucifixion with its prickly dark green leaves; as the Crown of Thorns and the Blood of Christ with its red berries.

Hope, Bob - Entertainer who held the first Christmas show for the soldiers overseas in 1941.

Horse - During the ancient Norse winter festival, Yule (Jul), the horse would be sacrificed to the god Woden or Odin. Until the 19th century, St. Nicholas rode a horse or a donkey or a sky chariot drawn by horses.

Hosanna - Hebrew for "We Pray," an exclamation of praise to God.

Hymn - The song of angels, a solemn song sung in High Latin and sternly theological with little or no emotional appeal. (Whereas, carols were sung in the common tongue and were happy, uplifting songs.)

𝔍𝔍

Icicles - Introduced from Nuremberg, Germany in 1878. Though originally introduced as silver foil strips, in 1920's were made of lead that would not tarnish. In 1960's made of mylar due to the potential of lead poisoning.
  • Legend has it that one cold winter night, the Christ child sought shelter in the forest and all the leaves had fallen but for the pine tree. When the pine tree realized he was caring for the Christ Child, tears of happiness fell and froze into icicles.

Immanuel (Emmanuel) - Hebrew for "God is with us." *Isaiah 7:14.*

Irving, Washington - American author who wrote *A History of New York,* a novel that introduced a number of Christmas traditions from Irving's European travels. Linked with Charles Dickens from England whose *A Christmas Carol* was written around the same time. These two authors formed the modern Christmas through their prose.

Ivy - Plant associated with the Greek god Bacchus - the Wine God. Eventually excluded from church celebrations due to the perception that unrestrained drinking and feasting took place when ivy displayed. Also the pagan symbol of eternal life.

J

Jehovah - Hebrew for "My Lord or God."

Jerusalem - Capital of Israel. The religious center of Christianity, Judaism and Islam.

Jeshau - Name given to Jesus by Mary and Joseph.

Jesus - Greek word for "to help" or "the help of God." Mary and Joseph named him Jeshau, which was the common Hebrew name meaning "the Lord is Salvation."

Joseph - Husband of Mary, the Mother of Christ. He was a carpenter from Nazareth, descendant of Bethlehem's David. When the priests recognized that the heavens smiled on Mary, they were given the task of choosing her husband. They summoned eligible men and ordered each to lay a bare branch on the altar. One branch burst into flower; it was held by Joseph.

Judah/Judea - Jerusalem was in Judah, the southern part of then ancient Palestine.

Jul (Yule) - Norse mid-winter festival. See *Yule*.

Julius I - Bishop of Rome 325 A.D., who declared December 25 as Christ's birthday. Not only (incorrectly) established the birth of Christ, but began the practice of the Church superimposing Christian festivals upon the pagan midwinter festivals.

K

Kalends - This was the Roman Holiday to commemorate the New Year. This Festival was celebrated from December 31 to January 6. Later, in 274 A.D., Emperor Aurelian declared a new holiday on December 25 to honor the goddess Myrtha, the latest Roman state religion. With both major holidays becoming established in ancient times, our modern 12 days of Christmas of December 25 to January 6 was established in this combination of these two ancient holidays. See *Christmas Day*.

Kermis - Dutch for "Christ Mass."

Khristkindle - German for "Christ Child." The name Khristkindle was "Americanized" to Kris Kringle, which is now a commonly used term for Santa Claus.

King Nutcracker - Guardian of the toys under the tree. See *Nutcracker*.

Kissing Ball - Made of evergreens, ornaments and mistletoe. Placed by the gentleman where the lady can easily overlook the Kissing Ball and be kissed.
See *Mistletoe*.

Kris Kringle - A term commonly used for Santa Claus, coming from the German word *Khristkindle* meaning "Christ Child."

𝕷

𝕷apps - Were the first people to depict Father Christmas or Santa Claus with a reindeer drawn sleigh.
See *Reindeer* and *Vladimir*.

Laurel (bay) - An herb and ancient symbol of triumph, also sacred to the god Apollo, the Roman Sun God. During the Christmas holiday used as a symbol of victory over sin and death.

Letters to Santa Claus - Began as an Advent tradition from Bavaria-Austria. The children would put little notes on the window sill on St. Nicholas Eve, December 5. They would be addressed to "dear child Jesus in Heaven" and St. Nicholas would pick them up and deliver them to the child Jesus.

Letters to Santa (which get replies) - Two services available:

Children write their cute letters and parents prepare a reply and enclose both letters, with a stamped, self addressed envelope to:
a) Santa's Mailbag; 354 OSS/OSW; 1215 Flightline Ave.; Suite 100B; Eielson AFB, AK 99702-1598
b) Santa Claus House; Santa Land, North Pole 99705*
*fee charged.

Lights on the Christmas Tree - Candles had been used for many years to represent the stars but, as the trees dried, the fire hazard became great. In 1882, Edward Johnson, a colleague of Edison's, had the first electrically lighted tree. Strings of light were begun by the Ever Ready Company in 1903. In 1927, General Electric introduced parallel wiring on its strings, which meant the entire chain would not go dark if one light failed. Twinkle lights were introduced in the 1970's.
See *Electric Lights/bulbs*.

Log Cakes - As the fireplace disappeared with the advent of central heating, cakes shaped like logs were used as a reminder of the yule log fire.

Lords of Misrule - In the early English celebrations, the church would appoint a Boy Bishop, chosen for good character. Symbolically these Boy Bishops were used as a release from normal social rules and would allow (symbolically) authority to be overturned, roles reversed. As time went on the Boy Bishops became Lords of Misrule as they took advantage and the situations would get out of hand, and chaos would reign. Elizabeth I saw the Boy Bishop as a tyrant and banned the practice.

Luke - One of the apostles who wrote of Christ's birth in the New Testament. His 2nd chapter set the scene. Luke 2: 1-20.

Luther, Martin (1483-1646) - Leader of the Reformation. Legend has it that as he was walking through the forest on Christmas Eve, he was overwhelmed by the natural beauty of the winter sky, stately evergreens and beautiful stars. As he tried to explain the glory of the scene to his family, words failed him. He cut down a small fir, placed candles on it, and began the Christmas tree tradition.

𝔐

𝔐agi - Indo-German meaning "great or illustrious" priestly scholars that specialized in science and astronomy. This priestly cast came from Persia and were considered Wise Men because they were able to interpret dreams. The Wise Men followed the Star of Bethlehem to become the first Gentiles to believe in Christ. Though the gospels did not mention the number of Wise Men, it did mention their three gifts. Caspar represented youth, Balthasar was middle age and Melchior the elderly. As they made this long trip, legend has it that they never replenished their food or water. They originally were interred at St. Sophia in Constantinople. After the 1st crusades, their remains were transferred to the Cathedral of Milan in 1164 A.D. Emperor Barbarassa soon conquered Milan and transferred their relics to Cologne, where they rest today. Refer to *Three Kings, Caspar, Balthasar, Melchior.*

Madonna - Olde Italian for "My Lady."

Manger - A feed box for animals. Used as a cradle for Christ. Possibly made of wood but more likely formed from potters clay and placed on a wooden support.

Mary - Mother of Christ and cousin of Elizabeth who was the mother of John the Baptist. Christ was conceived by the Holy Ghost and therefore Mary remained a virgin. This doctrine of Immaculate Conception was formally established in 649 A.D.

Matthew - One of the apostles whose Gospels began the Christmas celebrations. Matthew 2: 1-10.

Maypole - Originally made from the trunk of Christmas trees. Used on May 1st to celebrate the coming of spring.

Melchior - One of the Three Wise Men. He was the King of Arabia and Nubia and, as a 60 year old, represented the elders. As the "old man," he had white hair and a long beard. Brought gold in the form of a shrine representing royalty.

Merry - The original word meant "blessed, peaceful, pleasant" spiritual joys. Merry Christmas means "The Blessed Mass of Christ."

Merry Christmas in other languages:

Afrikaans	Een Plesierige Kerfes
Arabic	Idah saidan Wa Sanah Jaidah
Bohemian	Vesel Vanoe
Chinese	King Hsi Hsin Nien bing Chu Shen Tan
Croatian	Sretan Bozic
Czech	Vesel Vianoce
Dutch	Vrolyk Kerstfeest
English	Merry Christmas
Finnish	Houska Joula
French	Joyeux Noel
German	Froehlich Weihnachten
Greek	Genethlia
Hungarian	Lellemes Jarasconyi unnepeket
Irish	Nodlaig mhaith chugnat
Italian	Buon natale or Il Natale
Japanese	Meri Kurisumasu
Latin	Dies Natalis Domoni
Norwegian	Gledelig Jul
Philippino	Maligayang Pasko
Polish	Wesolych Swaiat or Narodzenie
Portuguese	Boas Festas or Natal
Russian	Rozhdestvo Khrista
Rumanian	Salbatori vesele
Serbian	Hristos se rodi
Spanish	Feliz Pacuas or La Navidad
Swedish	Glad Jul
Ukrainian	Srozhdestvom Kristovym
Welsh	Nadolog Llawen or Nadolig

Messiah - Hebrew for "the anointed one." When translated into Greek versions of the New Testament, the word was translated as *Khristos* from which the word "Christ" derives.

Micah - The prophet who foretold that the future ruler of Israel would come from Bethlehem; Micah 5:2.

Midnight Mass - Mass was celebrated at Midnight in the belief that this was the hour of Christ's birth; began around 400 A.D.

Mincemeat - The word itself comes from Middle French *nincer* "to cut in small pieces" (e.g. mince onions). These pies were originally called mutton pies made from lamb that represented the treasures of The Three Wise Men. They were baked in a loaf shape to resemble a manger.

Mincemeat Recipe: Enough for two 9-inch pies.

> *1/4 pound beef suet, ground*
> *1/2 cup light brown sugar*
> *2 cups raisins*
> *2 cups currants*
> *1 cup chopped almonds*
> *1 tart apple, peeled, cored and grated*
> *Grated rind and juice of 1 lemon*
> *1 teaspoon cinnamon*
> *1 teaspoon allspice*
> *1 teaspoon almond extract*
> *1/2 teaspoon mace or nutmeg*
> *1/2 teaspoon ground cloves*
> *1/2 cup apricot preserves*
> *1 cup brandy or applejack*
> *port wine (optional)*
>
> *Combine all the ingredients except the port wine in a bowl or crock with a lid. Cover, and leave in a cool place for 1 month. Stir the mixture once a week. Add a little port wine if the mixture seems too dry, though there should be sufficient brandy to keep it moist. Yields 2 quarts. Serve with ice cream. Or...*
> *To make 2 (9 inch) pies, put in unbaked pie crusts and cover with latticed (woven strips of) pie crust. Bake in preheated oven at 350 degrees for 1 hour or until crust is golden. (1 pie serves 8.)*

Mrs. Santa Claus - introduced by Katherine Lee Bates in her book *Good Santa Claus on a Sleigh Ride* in 1889.

Mistletoe - A parasitic plant that the ancient Druid priests believed to be
magical. It was one of the only plants to bear its fruit during the winter.
Because it was so highly treasured by this pagan Celtic culture, it was
considered sinful and pagan for the Church.
The Kissing tradition comes from a combination of several legends:
- Mistletoe was hung high because of the ancient belief that the plant
  should never touch the ground or bad luck would follow.
- It is a symbol of peace for the Romans who, if they met an enemy
  under the mistletoe, would lay aside their weapons, kiss each other and
  declare a truce until the next day.
- Yet another legend has it that mistletoe was the original tree used for
  Christ's cross; in its shame it shrunk to this parasitic shrub.
  Over the centuries, feelings about mistletoe have gone from sacred and
  magical to fun and playful. The kiss of peace has turned into a kiss of
  playfulness. See *Kissing Ball*.

Mithra/Myrtha - Persian god of light who drove away the dark during the Persian
mid-winter festivals. At one time a rival to Christianity, Mithraism
entered the Roman world around 1 B.C. and became an official State
religion by 274 A.D. That year Aurelian proclaimed a new holiday -
Natalis Solis Invictus - The Birthday of the Unconquered Sun to be
celebrated on *December 25*. Though it had many common components
with Christianity (baptism, sacramental meal, Sabbath, good versus
evil, defeat of evil by moral rectitude, salvation, heaven and hell), it
had the oriental tradition of no place for women and eventually was
superseded by Christianity. In 325 A.D. the Bishop of Rome, Julius I,
declared December 25 as Christ's birthday, superimposing Christian
festivals upon pagan midwinter festivals.

Moore, Clement (1779-1863) - American author most famous for his poem,
A Visit from St. Nicholas , published in 1824. This poem was credited
for developing the myth of the modern Santa Claus. Moore's Santa
Claus came from the traditions of America, Holland and Britain.
Examples:
- *chubby and plump* is the very opposite of the lean, ascetic bishop
  shown in medieval paintings;
- *right jolly old elf* is from the Jul elves of Scandinavian countries;
  dressed all in fur from his head to his foot is from the German
  Pelznickel;
- *laying his finger aside his nose* are taken from Washington Irving's
  *History of New York from the Beginning of the World to the End of the
  Dutch Dynasty.*

Music -

(All I want for Christmas is) My Two Front Teeth: Words and
  music by Don Gardner.
Angels We Have Heard on High: Traditional, possibly French.
Away in a Manger: Words by Martin Luther; music by
  Carl Mueller.
Blue Christmas: Words and music by Billy Hayes and
  Jay Johnson.
The Chipmunk Song: Words and music by Ross Bagdasarian.
The Christmas Song (Chestnuts roasting on an open fire):
  Words and music by Mel Torme and Robert Wells.
Deck the Halls: Traditional, possibly Welsh.
Do They Know It's Christmas: Words and music by M. Ure
  and B. Geldof.
The First Noel: Traditional, possibly English.
Frosty the Snow Man: Words and music by Steve Nelson and
  Jack Rollins.
Go, Tell It on the Mountain: Spiritual
God Rest Ye Merry Gentlemen: Traditional, possibly English.
Good King Wenceslaus: Words by John Neals; music, traditional.
Hark! The Angels Sing: Words by Charles Wesley; music by
  Felix Mendelssohn.
Have Yourself a Merry Little Christmas: Words and music by
  Hugh Martin and Ralph Blane.
Here Comes Santa Claus: Words and music by Gene Autry
  and Oakley Haldereman.
A Holly JollyChristmas: Words and music by Johnny Marks.
(There's no place like) Home for the Holidays: Words by Al
  Stillman, music by Robert Allen.
I Saw Mommy Kissing Santa Claus: Words and music by
  Johnny Marks.
I Saw Three Ships: Traditional, possibly English.
I'll be Home for Christmas: Words by Kim Gannon; music by
  Walter Kent.
It Came Upon a Midnight Clear: Words by Edmund Sears; music
  by Richard Wilis.
It's Beginning to Look a Lot Like Christmas: Words and music by
  Meredith Wilson.
Jingle-Bell Rock: Words and music by Joe Beal and Jim Boothe.
Jingle Bells: Words and music by James Pierpont.
Jolly Old St. Nicholas: Traditional.
Joy to the World: Words by Isaac Watts; music by Lowell Mason.
Let It Snow! Let It Snow! Let It Snow!: Words by Sammy Cahn;
  music by Jule Styne.

Music - (continued) -

The Little Drummer Boy: Words and music by Katherine Davis,
    Henry Onorati and Harry Simeone.
(The) Most Wonderful Day of the Year: Words and music by
    Johnny Marks.
My Favorite Things: Words Oscar Hammerstein; music
    Richard Rogers.
Nuttin' for Christmas: Words and music by Sid Tepper and
    Roy Bennett.
O Christmas Tree (O Tannenbaum) - Traditional, possibly
    German.
O Come, O Come, Emmanuel: Traditional, possibly French.
O Holy Night: Words by John Sullivan; music by Adolphe Adam.
O Little Town of Bethlehem: Words by Phillips Brooks; music by
    Lewis Redner.
Over the River and Through the Woods: Traditional.
Parade to the Toy Soldiers: Words by Ballard MacDonald; music
    by Leon Jessel.
Rockin' Around the Christmas Tree: Words and music by Johnny
    Marks.
Rudolph the Red-Nosed Reindeer: Words and music by Johnny
    Marks.
Santa Claus Is Comin' to Town: Words and music by J. Fred
    Coots and Haven Gillespie.
Silent Night: Words by Joseph Mohr; music by Franz Gruber.
Silver Bells: Words and music by Jay Livingston and Ray Evans.
Sleigh Ride: Words by Mitchell Paris; music by Leroy Anderson.
Twelve Days of Christmas: Traditional, possibly English.
ToyLand: Words by Glen MacDonough; music by Victor Herbert.
Up On the Housetop: Words and music by Benjamin Hanby.
We Three Kings of Orient Are: Words and music by John Hopkins.
We Wish You a Merry Christmas: Traditional, possibly English.
What Child Is This: Words by William Chatterton Dix; music
    traditional.
White Christmas: Words and music by Irving Berlin.

Myrrh - A gift to Christ from Balthasar, it is a resin from the sap of a tree. The
    tree is tapped and drained of its sap to develop this resin to make oils
    for perfumes. Derived from a thorny tree, considered a symbol of
    Jesus's suffering or his approaching sacrifice. Pragmatically, used to
    deter stable's vermin.

Mystery Plays (Miracle Plays) - They were used by the Church as a means of
    teaching the common people the basics of the scriptures. Since most
    people were illiterate, these plays were used to educate the peasants.

Nast, Thomas - German born illustrator who is given credit for creating the physical appearance of the modern Santa Claus. He began a series of illustrations in 1862 and, over the next 23 years, helped define the Santa Claus appearance as well as his surroundings (e.g. North Pole workshops, the great book in which all the children's names were recorded, an old-fashioned hand-held telescope with which to keep an eye on the world, etc.).

Nativity - Word used to describe the birth of Christ. From Latin word *natalis* or "day of birth" or "birthday."

Nativity Plays - Dramatized "miracle" plays used by the church to attract unsophisticated peasants from their pagan customs. St. Francis of Assisi is credited with using the first Nativity "scene" to depict the birth of Christ in 350 A.D.

Nativity Site - His birth site is at the Grotto of the Nativity, Bethlehem. It has changed little in 2000 years and its oral tradition kept the Nativity location accurate. The Cave was even pinpointed by pagans. Emperor Constantine, 326 A.D., began to build a basilica over and around the Grotto, and it is one of Christendom's oldest churches.

Nazareth - The city Mary and Joseph returned to after their two year exile in Egypt thereby fulfilling the words spoken through the prophets "He shall be called a Nazarene." (Matthew 2:23)

Nicholas of Patara - He was the Bishop of Myra in then Asia Minor, now Turkey. This 4th century Bishop is the basis for the gift-givers like Santa Claus, Father Christmas etc. St. Nicholas remains are in Bari, Italy. This man's traditions and legends were brought back to Europe by Dutch sailors. The name St. Nicholas in the Dutch language is Sinter Klass, which is an easy jump to Santa Claus in America.
See *Santa Claus* and *Saint Nicholas*.

Noel - Derived from Latin *natalis* means "day of birth" or "birthday". In French it is an expression of joy. Commonly used during the Christmas season as a word for carol.

No Christmas - During the Puritan period of controlling the Parliament, the
Feast of the Nativity of Christ was no longer celebrated. Between 1644
and 1656 Christmas was decreed an ancient superstition, and the
Puritans did their best to "officialize" Christmas out of business. This
was brought about by the Reformation and a turning away from "popery" and the human influence in the Christianty of the day. Since most
of the early settlers were Puritan, this policy was brought to America.
As a Massachusetts law from 1659 stated: "Anybody who is found
observing by abstinence from labor, feasting, or any other way, such
day as Christmas Day, shall pay for (e)very offence - five shillings."
See *Reformation, Puritans*.

North Pole - The home of Santa Claus and his workshop with its sleigh and
reindeer. Said to have been appropriated from *Christmas Man* by
Thomas Nast. Nast's grandson asserted that Thomas Nast chose the
North Pole because it was equidistant from most countries in the
Northern Hemisphere, where Santa Claus could work without
interruption and no one country could claim him as his own.

Nutcracker- Made famous in the Christmas tradition from Hoffman's
Nutcracker and the Mouse King play. Comes from Olde English
hnutu meaning "nut" and *cracian* meaning "cracker."
See *King Nutcracker*.

Odin - Norse god who flew the winter skies on an eight-footed horse named
Sleipnier. He would bring reward or punishment to the people of this
part of Europe. One of many tales leading to Santa's flying sleigh!
See *Lapps*.

On this date in history - See *Time Line*.

Ornaments - Colorful and unique objects used to decorate trees, furnishings,
rooms, etc. Germans used to cover apples with colored paper which
lead to the idea of colored balls. Horns and bells were used to scare
off evil spirits. Early trees had good spirits called fairies, later termed
angels. The earliest ornaments were edibles of the fruit kind, later
cookies, cakes and candies. Popcorn or *maize* came from the
Americas, along with the stringing of cranberries. Flowers and paper
provided the non-edibles. From the Latin *ornare* meaning "to adorn."

Pageant - Comes from the word *pagonds*, wagons that were used to draw threatical stages around early Europe. These "shows" were the stories of Christmas and Easter and were used to help the peasants grasp the meaning of their religion.

Paradise Tree - In the German "miracle plays," The Garden of Eden was represented by a pine tree hung with apples. This "Tree of Life" depicted the creation of man and his demise from The Garden. The apples illustrated the sin of Adam and Eve. Later small white wafers were added to represent the Holy Ecuharist. Together, the tree bore both the fruit of sin (the apple) and also the saving fruit (the wafers).

Pelznickel - "Fur-Nicholas" - a combination of St. Nicholas and a little pagan companion that St. Nicholas would employ to issue reprimands to naughty children. He had a white beard, old clothes trimmed in fur, bags of toys for good children, and a rap with a switch for the naughty.

Piggy Bank - Derived from Boxing Day traditions. An earthenware container shaped like a pig that was filled with coins and money and was broken open on Boxing Day (December 26). The money saved through the year was given to the poor.

Piñata - Originating from Spain and Mexico, this paper-maché animal-shaped container is hung from the ceiling. It is filled with sweets and small toys. Blind-folded children are given a stick and three chances to whack the piñata, and once a solid whack connects, the goodies spill to the floor.

Pine Tree - One of the more important symbols of the Christmas season. Listed below are several legends that lend this symbol to the Christmas traditions:
- The ancient Druids sacrificed to the god Thor. St. Boniface interceded when the Druids were about to sacrifice a little child. He felled a sacred huge oak being used as an altar. The awestruck Druids listened to the story of Christ. St. Boniface, pointing close by to a little pine tree, told the Druids to take this tree and decorate it gaily and rejoice; to celebrate!
- Martin Luther was one of the originators of the Reformation, a religious movement away from the strong Roman Pope influence and a return to a biblical base for religious beliefs and ceremonies. As he was walking through the Black Forest he was overcome with the the majesty of the night. As he tried to explain his vision to his family and couldn't, he cut a small fir tree and set lighted candles upon it to represent the stars and the strength of nature that night.
See *Reformaton* and *Luther, Martin*.

Pine Tree - (continued)-

- When Christ was born, the birds, beasts and plants came to offer gifts.
  The pine tree, had none so God saw his disappointment and sent stars
  down to rest on it branches.
  See *Fir Tree* and *Tree*.

Pisces - An ancient astronomical sign when Mars, Jupiter and Saturn formed a
  triangle. Studies suggest this happened in the spring of 7 B.C. or 6
  B.C. and could have been what the Magi saw as the Star of Bethlehem.
  It is a symbol of high hopes and high ideals; it was also the astrological
  sign of Moses.

Plum Pudding - Though now uses raisins, original ingredients were
plums, prunes and meats.

1 (15-ounce) box, (2 1/2 cups) golden raisins
1 (15-ounce) box, (2 1/2 cups) dark raisins
1 (15-ounce) box, (2 1/2 cup) currants
2 cups mixed fruit rinds
1 1/2 cups chopped glazed cherries
1 1/2 cups slivered almonds
1 tart cooking apple, peeled, cored and grated
Grated rind of 2 oranges
2 teaspoons allspice
2 teaspoons cinnamon
1 tablespoon ground nutmeg
1 teaspoon ground cloves
1 teaspoon baking soda
1 teaspoon salt
1 cup flour
5 cups freshly made bread crumbs
2 1/2 cups firmly packed light brown sugar
4 eggs, lightly beaten
3 tablespoons molasses
1 cup Brandy or dark rum
Additional Brandy if needed.

*Put all ingredients, except additional brandy, into a very large mixing
bowl and mix them together with your hands. Butter the insides of
5 (1-quart) molds or bowls; divide mixture between them. Cover with
double thickness of aluminum foil and tie securely with string. Put
molds/bowls in roaster pan or similar container and add sufficient
boiling water to come three-quarters of way up sides. Cover container
with foil. Cook over low heat for 4 hours, refilling water as needed. Let
puddings cook in water. When cool, store in cool place for a month or
more, adding Brandy from time to time.*
*Reheat puddings by steaming them in same "double boiler" and cook-
ing for 2 hours. Heat 2 ounces Brandy in small saucepan and put hot
puddings on rimmed plate. Pour on Brandy, light, and serve flaming.
Yield: 5 (1 quart) puddings.*

Poinsettia - Ornamental shrub from Mexico. *Flor de la Nache Buena*, "The
Flower of the Natviity" or "Flower of the Holy Night." Brought to the
United States by the first Ambassador, Dr. Joel Poinsette in 1852.
  • In Mexico, it is traditional to leave gifts before the creche in the church
  on Christmas Eve. Legend has it that a poor boy, having nothing to
  give, knelt and prayed. A beautiful scarlet plant immediately grew and
  he presented it as his gift to the Christ Child. The poinsettia is thought
  to resemble the Star of Bethlehem.

Pomanders - Popular homemade presents of apples, oranges, lemons or limes. Stick each fruit all over with cloves and roll in a mixture of cinnamon, allspice, orris root, cardamom and ginger. Tie coated fruit with red or green ribbon and hang to dry.

Prange, Louis - The "Father of the American Christmas Card."

Presidents and the Christmas Tree -

1856 Franklin Pierce introduced the first fir tree to the White House.
1895 Grover Cleveland first to use electric lights.
1923 Calvin Coolidge began lighting The National Community Christmas Tree.

Puritans - When they dominated the English Parliament from 1644 to 1656 they wanted to "purify" the festivals of Christmas and the "relics of Popery" and saw Christmas totally without Biblical sanctions. They sought and achieved the banning of Christmas as a "religious" holiday, and it was not reinstated until 1660 under Charles II.
See *No Christmas*.

Pyramid (Christmas) - The forerunner to the Christmas Tree in Germany. Many candles were placed on a pyramid made of shelves of graduated widths until a pyramid shape unit was complete.

℗

Quakers - Early Pennsylvania settlers who were scornful of the Christmas celebrations, and were as adamant as the Puritans in not celebrating.

Queen Victoria - German born Prince Albert, husband to the Queen, established the German Christmas tree tradition in England. The Prince sorely missed his homeland traditions of the family Christmas Tree. In 1840 the Royal Family decked the halls of Windsor Castle and celebrated with a Royal Family Tree for the first time. Once becoming a "royal tradition," it gradually filtered to the common people of the United Kingdom, then it became a common practice in America.

Reformation - Around 1547, one of the tenets of this major religious movement was the Puritan disapproval of the Christmas celebrations. These Puritans believed that the ceremonial customs were getting out of hand; not only did they disapprove of the nativity but Christmas itself. As Oliver Cromwell's political power grew in the English Parliament, laws were passed to outlaw the Christmas holiday ceremonies. This influence came to America with the earliest settlers, and, by 1659, the Puritans in America enacted laws to declare no observations of Christmas under penalty of fines. This attitude prevailed well into the 19th century.

Regal Gifts of the Magi :

Gold (precious metal) - to ease Mary's poverty; symbol of Christ as King of the World.

Frankincense (sweet resin) - to ward off aroma of stable; symbol of Christ as King of Heaven.

Myrrh (from thorny tree) - to deter stable vermin; symbol of Christ's approaching sacrifice.

Restoration - After a given amount of time, the religious pendulum eventually swung back to, among other things, the celebrating of Christ's birth, and the return to Christmas festivities.

Reindeer - Belief that this part of the modern Christmas tradition began in Lappland, an area in Russia. The Lapps used domesticated reindeer as the only means of transporting sleigh loads with great speed. With the legend of St. Nicholas being brought to Russia by Peter the Great, St. Nicholas was transposed from riding a donkey to riding in a sleigh. This Lappland tradition crossed the borders of the Scandinavian traditions. American author Clement Moore incorporated the sleigh ride into his famous poem *A Visit from St. Nicholas* and the German-American illustrator Thomas Nast used the reindeer-pulled sleigh as part of his "history" of St. Nicholas in *Harpers Weekly* magazine. The name itself comes from the Olde Norse *herinn* meaning "reindeer," shortened into Olde English as *rein* coupled with *dyr* meaning "deer" coupled together to form "reindeer." See *Lapps* and *Vladimir*.

Reindeer names - Blitzen, Comet, Cupid, Dancer, Dasher, Donner, Prancer, Vixen and, later, *Rudolph the Red-Nosed Reindeer.*

Rosemary (bush) - *Mary's Rose* - Represents man's redemption from Adam's fall. As the Holy Family fled Herod they stopped by a stream to wash their garments, and spread them to dry on the Rosemary bush. From that moment the bush was blessed with a delicate fragrance. In the middle-ages it was spread on the floor, and as people walked and danced, a pleasant aroma arose to fill the room.

Royal Family - Queen Victoria and Prince Albert began the family Christmas tradition in England. Prince Albert was from Germany and brought the German custom of a family Christmas tree to England and from there it went to America.

Rudolph the Red-Nosed Reindeer - In 1939, copywriter Robert May was assigned to write a give-away booklet for Montgomery Ward and over 2 million were given away. It was reissued in 1946 when another 3 million were given away. May's songwriter friend, Johnny Marks, wrote the music and it was first recorded by Gene Autry in 1949.

Saint Augustine - Introduced Christianity to England in 600 A.D. St. Augustine had questioned Pope Gregory on how to convert the Druids to Christianity. The Pope advised "...to accommodate the ceremonies of the Christian Churches as much as possible to those of the heathen," thus continuing the Churches supplanting of strong pagan festivals with Church holidays.

Saint Andrew - One of the Twelve Disciples and the brother of Peter. Patron Saint of Scotland and Russia whose Feast Day is November 30. See *Advent.*

Saint Barbara - The Anniversary of her martyrdom is celebrated on December 4. This date is the traditional day in Syria and Lebanon to start their Christmas celebrations. The table is lit with candles, wheat flour cakes set out, and a procession made around the table while chanting the festival songs opens the festivities.

Saint Boniface - Completed the Christianization of Germany. Introduced the custom of linking pagan tree worship with everlasting life as symbolized by evergreens. Circa 675. See *Winfred.*

Saint Cyril (of Jerusalem) - Requested that Pope Julius I investigate the most probable time of Christ's birth.

Saint Francis (of Assissi) - Introduced the use of the "crib" or Nativity to instruct the poor, uneducated masses about the story of Christmas in1223 A.D. Using living animals and students to teach, this "act" or "play" was to instill forever, in the hearts of the peasants, the story of Christ's birth.

Saint Gregory (Pope Gregory I) - Was asked by St. Augustine on how to convert the Ancient Druids to Christianity. Pope Gregory advised: "...to accommodate the ceremonies of Christian Churches, as much as possible to those of the heathen," thereby furthering the Churches use of supplanting pagan mid-winter festivals into the now official Roman religion.

Saint Lucia - Celebrated in Sweden on December 13. The oldest daughter of the household wears a white dress with a red sash and a crown of lighted candles on her head. The tradition is for her to serve coffee, buns and breakfast snacks to her parents as the household awakens.

Saint Luke - One of the apostles whose gospels began the Christmas traditions. Chapter 2 1:20. Circa 1st century.

Saint Matthew - One of the apostles whose gospels began the Christmas traditions. Chapter 2 1:10. Circa 1st century.

Saint Martins - Early Christian patron of wines and vintners. Bonfires were lighted on the eve of his day November 11. The animals that could not be fed for the winter were slaughtered and salted down. It was a day of feasting when the first of the new wines were drunk.

Saint Nicholas - Though the best loved of the Christmas spirits and legends, there truly was a St. Nicholas. He was from the ancient city Myra, located in then Asia Minor, now Turkey. He became the Boy Bishop of Myra, and was persecuted by Emperor Diocletian then was released by Constantine the Great. St. Nicholas died on December 6, 343 A.D. This is the history of the man, but there are also the myths and legends. For example, He is remembered for saving three daughters from certain prostitution. Their father, a destitute nobleman, could not afford the dowry expected of a man of that caste. As the daughters came of marriageable age, on three different occasions, he went at night to their house, and threw bags of gold coins down the chimney so that each daughter could enter into an honorable marriage. This act of kindness evolved into the legend of St.Nicholas being able to enter the home through the chimney. Though his roots reach to ancient man, he has been so popularized through the ages that he inspires the people of today from so long ago. As his legends and myths grew out of his homeland and into the rest of Europe, he became important enough to become part of the Christmas celebrations.
See *Nicholas of Patara*.

Evolution of name Santa Claus from St. Nicholas:

Latin	Sanctus Nicolaus
Dutch	Sinter Nikolaas (Sinter Klaas)
"Americanized"	Santa Claus

Saint Patrick - Circa 385. As the patron Saint of Ireland he is credited with
    bringing Christianity and Christmas to this country. Though his
    Feast day is March 17, in his home country, he is revered at the
    Christmas holidays.

Saint Stephen - Circa 35. Was the first Irish martyr whose day is celebrated on
    December 26. In England, it is Boxing Day when the alms boxes for the
    poor are opened and distributed.
    See *Boxing Day*.

Santa Claus - He is the American adaptation of St. Nicholas, but in America he
    is no longer a bishop but a combination of Father Christmas from
    England, St. Nicholas from the Netherlands and other legends from
    Europe. For instance the ascetic robes of the Bishop gave way to the
    secular dress of Father Christmas. He went from a tall lanky Father
    Christmas to a short chubby man with a long beard from the Dutch.
    His Bishop's miter (cap) changed to a fir trimmed hat and suit coming
    from the influence of Bavaria by way of Thomas Nast. From using
    a gray donkey or a white horse, he was transported by the famously
    named reindeer thanks to Clement Moore. To use the term of the
    nineties, he has been "morphed" into what we see today from
    thousands of years in development. See *Saint Nicholas* and
    Nicholas of Patara.

Saturnalia - A week long Roman pagan festival to the god Saturn, representing
    plenty and bounty. This was the main festival associated with the
    winter solstice-THE holiday of the year. Ancient man began this holiday
    on December 17, then the festival date was moved to December 25 to
    celebrate the official Roman religion, Mirthaism. This new celebration
    was for The Birthday of the Unconquered Sun, which was the principal
    feast-day of this Mithraic religion. This pagan festival is the forerunner
    of the winter holidays we celebrate today.

Savior - Hebrew for "One who saves or delivers."

Seals - Through a voluntary donation you purchase these holiday stamps (not
    for postage) to decorate Christmas card envelopes. In 1904 Einar
    Holbell Danis began the Christmas Seals in Denmark to campaign
    against tuberculosis. Introduced in America by John Riis, a Danish
    immigrant in 1904.

Septuagint - Most influential Greek version of Old Testament. As this Torah (Old Testament) traveled from East to West around the Mediterranean Sea, from Palestine, to Greece, to Rome, translations were needed as it traveled. For example "Messiah," a Hebrew term for "anointed one," was translated into Greek with the word *Khristos* from which Christ derives. Such is the evolution of words and their effect on history. See *Christ*.

Shepherds - Sheep herders who are very intricate to the Christmas tapestry. It was the shepherds who were to know of His birth first, when the angel of the Lord came to them as they watched their flocks and said *"...fear not, for behold, I bring you tidings of great joy, which shall be to all people. For unto you is born this day, in the City of David, a saviour, which is Christ the Lord. And this shall be a sign unto you. Ye shall find the babe wrapped in swaddling clothes, laying in a manger."* The shepherds were the first to visit the Christ Child.

Sleigh - A vehicle on runners that can travel though the snow. From the Dutch word *slee* or *sled*; also from Olde English where *sled* meant "to slide."

Solstice - *Where the sun stands still*. The Winter Solstice, December 21, is the shortest, cruelest day and the longest night of the year. From time before memory, in order to help the sun god relight his lamp, ancient peoples feasted and rejoiced as the sun began its return on December 22. Ancient man began his festivities of rebirth with prayers and ceremonies, adorning their homes with holly, ivy, mistletoe and evergreens, all the plants that withstood the death of winter. For our ancients, this time of year was devoted to harvests, hearth and fire. Here is where the ideas and themes of rebirth, harvest and light were born into our modern traditions. All the winter festivals came from this date (the shortest day, the longest night) with the petitioning of the gods that the sun may return.

Spider(s) - From the Ukraine, where trees were decorated with cobwebs. Symbolic folk tale in which a spider decorated a poor man's Christmas tree on Christmas Eve. When the family awoke, Jesus had turned the spider web into silver. See *tinsel*.

Star of Bethlehem - Star of the East or Christmas Star. Though a central part of the Christmas pageant, the star mentioned in the Bible remains a mystery. With much of the debate centering around the myth versus facts, the following possibilities are offered as explanations:

- Biblical or supernaturalist view is seen as literal history: *"The star, which they saw in the east, went before them, till it came and stood over where the young child was."* A creator (God) kindled event.

- Rationalists: The story is a myth or symbolic at best. A mythical, spiritual light or simply outside the domain of science, it is now a part of the interwoven story we now call Christmas.

- Historical (four possibilities):

  □ Great Meteor, but this is such a short event that it could not be the star.
  □ Comet, more tenable, as Chinese records indicate in the spring of 4 B.C., February to March, there was such a comet.
  □ New temporary Star - not likely.
  □ Conjunction of known stars and planets, also tenable for in 7 B.C. or 6 B.C., Jupiter, Saturn and Mars were aligned, but not much weight given to this hypothesis, as any part of the globe could see it, not just Bethlehem. See *Pisces*.

Stockings - In the olden days, stockings were not a common item, so they were washed almost daily and hung to dry by the chimney. To confirm why we attach so much significance to them as gift holders, they actually represent the wooden shoes from the Dutch children's tradition of placing the shoes at the door on St. Nicholas' Eve night to receive the presents that might be given by St. Nicholas or his servant, Black Peter. In America and England, traditionally an apple is placed in the toe for good health and, in the heel, an orange and a nut.

Straw - Used as ancient appeal to the spirits for good harvests and a reminder of the Bethlehem stable.

Sugar Plums - A traditional recipe for *"...visions of sugar plums danced in their heads"*...from Clement Moore

1 cup dried apricots	*2 cups vanilla wafers*
1 cup pecans	*1 cup flaked coconut*
1/2 cup pitted dates	*1/2 cup orange juice*
1/2 cup golden raisins	*1/2 cup sugar*

Finely chop the apricots, pecans, dates and raisins in food processor or with a knife. Use rolling pin to crush wafers in a plastic bag (making sure you have 1 cup crumbs). Place fruit, nut and crumbs in a large bowl and toss with coconut and orange juice. Form 1 inch balls; roll ball in sugar. Place in cups or wrap with paper and tie tops with ribbon or cord. Yield: About 6 dozen "sugar plums."

Sundblom, Haddon - An artist who updated Santa Claus for the 20th Century. In 1931, he began a series of Santa Claus paintings commissioned by The Coca-Cola Company. His description varied little from the Thomas Nast era, but made Santa a robust, grandfather figure, now well over 6 feet tall, no longer the elfin figure of yore.

Swaddling Clothes - Long narrow bands of cloth wrapped around a baby infant. Used in ancient times to restrict its movement.

𝕋

Tannenbaum - German for "fir tree."

Three Kings - Magi - Wise Men - The ancient priests who traveled to Bethlehem in search of the King of the Jews. It was believed that they came from an observatory at the Hill of Vaus, India. The three priests were named Melchior, (who brought gold, a symbol of sovereignty), Caspar (who brought Frankincense, a symbol of divinity), and Balthazar (who brought myrrh a symbol of humanity). In addition to the sight of the Star of Bethlehem as a sign of the Savior's arrival, legend has it, at the midnight hour of Christ's birth, an ostrich kept by Caspar hatched two eggs, one yielding a lion and the other a lamb. Melchior had a bird fly into his garden and announce the birth of Christ in a human voice. To Balthazar was born a son with the power of speech fully developed. The child told that Jesus's mother would be a virgin and that He would live for 33 years, while Bathazar's son himself would only survive 33 days. After their visit to Bethlehem, the place they had sought, they traveled to Sewa (now Turkey) where death awaited. Melchior died at 169 years of age on January 1. Balthazar at 149 on January 6 and Caspar at 109 on January 11, all in the year 54 A.D.
See *Magi, Caspar, Melchior, Balthasar.*

Time Line - "On this Date in History" and "just for the fun of it!"

*Took place on December 25.

1200 B.C. and before - Ancient man celebrated the winter solstice the world over. (Approximately December 21)

274 B.C. Romans celebrate Saturnalia, The Invincible Sun, on December 25.

0 A.D. Birth of Christ.

2 A.D. Joseph and Mary return to Nazareth.

33 A.D. Christ dies.

66 A.D. Druids and Celts defeated by Romans.

*336 A.D. First recorded celebration of Christmas on December 25.

350 A.D. St. Nicholas becomes Bishop.

*496 A.D. Clovis, King of Franks was baptized with 3000 of his men.

500 A.D. Pope Gregory declares December 25 as Christ's birth.

*521 A.D. Legend holds that King Arthur feasted and obtained his magic sword Excalibur.

532 A.D. Monk Exgius starts Christian system of dates.

*800 A.D. Charlemagne crowned Holy Roman Emperor.

*1066 A.D. William The Conqueror crowned King of England.

1100 A.D. Baldwin of Edessa revived crown of Latin Kingdom of Jerusalem after brief success of 1st crusade.

*1223 A.D. St. Francis of Assisi assembled the first Nativity scenes in Greccio, Italy.

1350 A.D. Boxing Days begin.

*1492 A.D. Columbus' ship, the Santa Maria, sinks.

*1539 A.D. Hernando DeSoto celebrates first Christmas in New World.

1542 A.D. First turkey imported to Europe.

1648 A.D. Cromwell comes to power in Parliament.

*1759 A.D. George Washington and Martha marry.

*1776 A.D. General George Washington crosses Delaware.

*1818 A.D. First performance of *Silent Night*.

1824 A.D. *A Visit from St. Nick* written by Clement Moore.

1827 A.D. Thomas Nast publishes first *Jolly Santa Claus* and introduces the illiustrations of the modern Santa.

1841 A.D. Queen Victoria has family tree in Windsor castle.

1843 A.D. Charles Dickens publishes *A Christmas Carol*.

1843 A.D. First Christmas card by John Horsley.

1856 A.D. President Pierce has first White House Tree.

*1868 A.D. President Johnson pardons Confederate States.

1875 A.D. Louis Prange prints first American Christmas card.

1892 A.D. Tchaikovsky writes *"The Nutcracker."*

1897 A.D. *"Yes! Virginia there is a Santa Claus"* published.

*1914 A.D. WWI "unofficial" Christmas truce along no man's land.

Time Line - (continued) -

1923 A.D. President Coolidge has first tree on White House lawn.
* 1926 A.D. Hirohito becomes Emperor of Japan.
* 1927 A.D. First Macy's Day Parade.
*1936 A.D. Chiang Kai-shek released from kidnapping.
*1937 A.D. 1st Post Office Christmas stamp issued in Austria.
1939 A.D. Poem *Rudolph Red-Nosed Reindeer* written.
*1941 A.D. Hong Kong surrenders to Japan.
*1946 A.D. Battle of the Bulge begins in WWII.
1962 A.D. United States Post Office first Christmas stamp issued.

Tinsel - Ornaments for Christmas trees. From the French word *entincelle* meaning "to sparkle." The English shortened it to "tinsel" where it became a kind of cloth made of silk or satin woven with strands of gold or silver.
  • The legend: The spiders loved to decorate the Christmas trees, but their cobwebs could only be seen from the ground, so they covered the entire tree with cobwebs. When the Christ child came to bless the tree, he touched the webs and they turned to silver. See *Spiders*.

Tiny Tim - A character from Charles Dickens *A Christmas Carol*; Bob Cratchit's crippled son.

Tree - Ultimate Guide:
  Preparing - Know dimensions; have rope, blankets for car protection, gloves.
  Choosing - Fresh shipments only; do during the daylight so you can see tree shape; smell, view all angles.
  Freshness - Slam tree trunk down, should be few needles on ground; slide hand on branches (needles should stay).
  Making it last - Take one inch from bottom to break sap seal, put into water once home, keep water levels full.
  Safety - Unplug lights when replacing and when family will be away for extended time; notice dryness of needles; keep away from heat sources; check wiring for fraying.
  Recycling - Municipal programs, use loppers.
  See *Fir Tree*.

Turkey - One of the few North American contributions to the Christmas celebrations. This bird came from North America to Spain around 1518 and returned to America as part of our Christmas festivities.

Twelve Days of Christmas - From Christmas, December 25, to The Epiphany on January 6. The cycle of birth to baptism.

Twelve Days of Christmas (song) - It's origins are from Medieval French
troubadours. Formally published by Englishman J.O. Helliwell in 1842.

First the song itself and then two interpretations:

On the 1st day of Christmas my true love sent to me:
A partridge in a pear tree
2 turtle doves
3 French hens
4 calling birds (See colly)
5 gold rings
6 geese a-laying
7 swans a-swimming
8 maids a-milking
9 ladies dancing
10 lords a-leaping
11 pipers piping
12 drummers drumming.

Interpretation A:

Date	Poem
12/26	Partridge - Delicacy for 1st day of festivities.
12/27	2 turtle doves - Symbol of love.
12/28	3 French hens - More than likely not birds but stone wine bottles.
12/29	4 colly birds (not calling) - Colly is French for "black" so may read 4 black birds as in 4 and 20 blackbirds from Old King Cole.
12/30	5 gold rings - Pope Innocent III sent four gold rings to King John representing the four virtues of a monarch: justice, fortitude, prudence, temperance, and, the fifth ring, love.
12/31	6 geese a-laying - Not for eating but for laying eggs for the cakes to come.
1/1	7 swans a-swimming - Unlike today where a swan is rarely eaten, in Queen Victoria's era it was common.
1/2	8 maids a-milking - Medieval lords showed their wealth and position by the extravagance of their feasts; all that cooking demanded a supply of milk, cream and butter.
1/3	9 ladies dancing - Clearly the celebration continues as the merriment continues.
1/4	10 lords a-leaping - From the Lord of Misrule where roles of servants and master reversed.
1/5	11 pipers piping - Medieval pipe or flute.
1/6	12 drummers drumming - Evil spirits were scared of sudden, loud noises. The last day of the Christmas celebraton, the day the evergreens and trees were removed to avert bad luck; a final opportunity for making merry.

Interpretation B:

12 drummers drumming	- Indicate the 12 articles of faith.
11 pipers piping	- Refer to the eleven apostles less Judas.
10 lords a-leaping	- Signify the Ten Commandments.
9 ladies dancing	- To recall the fruits of the Holy Spirit: love, joy, peace, long-suffering, gentleness, goodness, faith, meekness, and temperance.
8 maids a-milking	- Represents the Beatitudes, declarations from Sermon on the Mount.
7 swans a-swimming	- Indicates the gifts of the Holy Spirit: piety, wisdom, counsel, fear of the Lord, understanding, knowledge and fortitude.
6 geese a-laying	- Are the six days of creation, or six days of humanity's labors before the Sabbath.
5 gold rings	- First five books of the Old Testament.
4 calling birds	- Gospels of Matthew, Mark, Luke, and John.
3 French hens	- Symbolize the three gifts of the Magi; or faith, hope and charity.
2 turtle doves	- Stand for the two birds sacrificed by the Jews at the birth of a son.
a partridge in a pear tree	- The bird represents Christ, who gathers his young under his wings.

Ⓤ

United States of America - It is a giant melting pot of all Christmas traditions. We adopted the ways that pleased us and, by the end of the 19th century, Christmas became a dual holiday, embracing religious as well as folk celebrations. The American media and culture have such a dominant impact on our Christmas traditions, from over-commercialization to the elimination of St. Nicholas "dark servant," that we have assembled bits and pieces from the conglomerate of the world to the colorful celebration we now have.

𝔙

Virgin Birth - Not only found in Christian religions, but in Jewish
    religion with the birth of Isaac. New Testament tells of
    the conception of Jesus by the Holy Spirit and this was
    generally accepted by the 2nd century.

Virgin Mary - See *Mary.*

A Visit from St. Nick by Clement Moore

> *T'was the night before Christmas, when all through the house*
> *Not a creature was stirring, not even a mouse,*
> *The stockings were hung by the chimney with care,*
> *In hopes that St. Nicholas soon would be there;*
> *The children were nestled all snug in their beds;*
> *While visions of sugar-plums danced in their heads;*
> *And Mamma in her 'kerchief, and I in my cap,*
> *Had just settled our brains for a long winter's nap,*
> *When out on the lawn there arose such a clatter,*
> *I sprang from the bed to see what was the matter*
> *Away to the window I flew like a flash,*
> *Tore open the shutters and threw up the sash.*
> *The moon on the breast of the new-fallen snow*
> *Gave the luster of midday to objects below,*
> *When, what to my wondering eyes should appear,*
> *But a miniature sleigh, and eight tiny reindeer.*
> *With a little old driver, so lively and quick,*
> *I knew in a moment it must be St. Nick.*
> *More rapid than eagles his coursers they came,*
> *And he whistled, and shouted, and called them by name:*
> *Now, Dasher! now Dancer! now Prancer and Vixen!*
> *On, Comet! on, Cupid! on Donner and Blitzen!*
> *To the top of the porch! to the top of the wall!*
> *Now dash away! dash away! dash away all!*
> *As dry leaves that before the wild hurricane fly,*
> *So up to the house-top the coursers they flew,*
> *With the sleigh full of toys, and St. Nicholas too.*
> *And then, in a twinkling, I heard on the roof,*
> *The prancing and pawing of each little hoof.*
> *As I drew in my head, and was turning around*
> *Down the chimney St. Nicholas came with a bound.*
> *He was dressed all in fur, from his head to his foot,*
> *And his clothes were all tarnished with ashes and soot;*
> *A bundle of toys he had flung on his back,*
> *And he looked like a peddler just opening his pack.*
> *His eyes-how they twinkled! His dimples how merry!*
> *His cheeks were like roses, his nose like a cherry!*

His droll little mouth drawn up like a bow,
And the beard on his chin was as white as the snow;
The stump of a pipe he held tight in his teeth,
And the smoke it encircled his head like a wreath;
He had a broad face and a little round belly ,
That shook when he laughed, like a bowlful of jelly.
He was chubby and plump, a right jolly old elf,
And I laughed when I saw him, in spite of myself;
A wink of his eye and a twist of his head
Soon gave me to know I had nothing to dread.
He spoke not a word, but went straight to his work,
And filled the stockings; then turned with a jerk,
And laying his finger aside of his nose,
And giving a nod, up the chimney he rose;
He sprang to his sleigh, to his team gave a whistle,
And away they all flew like the down of a thistle.
But I heard him exclaim, ere he drove out of sight.
Happy Christmas to all and to all a good night.

Vladimir - A Russian Emperor who captured the legend of St. Nicholas while
visiting Constantinopole. Within Russia there is a large territory known
as Siberia and within Siberia is the Lapplands. The Lappland people
were known as the "people of reindeer sleds." The reindeer tradition
crossed the Swedish border and became part of the modern
Christmas story.
See *Lapps and Reindeer.*

𝔴

𝔴assail - In the American Christmas tradition, Wassail relates directly to the
Christmas Punch Bowl. From the English ritual of "Wassailing" or
partying, we derive the festive atmosphere of our own Christmas
parties. Originally an English drink related to the apple harvest, it
quickly evolved into a mid-winter ritual with a great deal of noise made
to ward off evil, or to signal the partying to begin. From Olde English,
o waes hael meaning "good health."

Wassail Punch - recipe:

6 apples for baking   *1/2 cup water*
1/2 cup apple juice   *1/2 gallon apple cider*
1/4 cup brown sugar   *2 1/2 cups cranberry or apricot juice*
Spice mixture of: 1 whole nutmeg, 2 whole cloves, 3 allspice
berries, 1 stick cinnamon, broken

Core apples and peel a narrow strip around top of each; place in
small baking dish. Pour apple juice in saucepan, add brown
sugar and bring to a boil. Pour mixture over apples and cover pan
with foil. Bake for 30 minutes at 350 degrees.   (Continued...)

Drain syrup from apples. Add water to syrup and place mixture in
saucepan. Mix spices together and enclose in cheesecloth bag.
Place tied spice bag in reserved syrup and water mixture and simmer
for 15 minutes. Stir in apple cider and cranberry or apricot juice.
Heat until mixture is steaming. Remove spice bag, pour
into punch bowl and float apples of top. Yield: 2 1/2 quarts.

Weir, Robert - In 1937 drew the first American portrait of Santa Claus based on his enthusiasm for Clement Moore's poem *A Visit from St. Nick.* He drew a Santa Claus as a short beardless man dressed in high boots, short coat and stocking cap. He had a frightening sneer, a sack overflowing with toys for good children and switches for bad, plus other added flourishes Weir could imagine from this famous poem.

Wenceslaus - Born in the 10th century, the Good King of Bohemia was martyred at 21 by his "pagan" brother Boleslav.

White Christmas - Most popular Christmas song ever. Written by Irving Berlin for the movie *Holiday Inn* and sung by Bing Crosby.

Winfred (St. Boniface) - He was an 8th century English missionary to Germany. On Christmas Eve he found idol worshipers (Druids) gathered around a large oak tree known as The Oak of Geismar (Blood Oak of Sacrifice) preparing to sacrifice Prince Asulf to the pagan god Thor. With a single stroke of his cross he felled the oak and behind the giant tree was a small fir tree. Winfred called it "The Tree of Life," a symbol of Jesus Christ. From that moment the fir tree became both a symbol of Christianity and a symbol of life.

Wise Men - See *Magi* and *Three Kings.*

Worship - The Magi were seeking a king, not a god. The Magi "fell down and worshipped him" could simply suggest the homage to a great ruler. The belief in Christ's divinity came slowly.

Wreath - To the Romans, wreathes were symbols of victory and honor, signs of peace and welcome. From Olde English *writhan* meaning "to twist." A wreath is circular, symbolizing both the love of God and the eternal joys of heaven.

Wreath, Advent - Came into common usage in the 16th century. Sometimes called the Advent Ring, it also contained the traditional evergreens but without mistletoe. The Germans use a horizontal wreath to hold the four candles for each consecutive Sunday.

X

X(mas)-from the Greek 'chi' sound. The Greek symbol chi is written by an X, and the Greek rho is used to identify the Christ figure and (phonetically) chi-rho or Khristos thus Xmas does stand for Christmas.

Y

Yes, Virginia-There is a Santa Claus

First printed in *New York Sun*, September 21, 1897:

We take pleasure in answering at once and thus prominently the communication below, expressing at the same time our great gratification that its faithful author numbered among the friends of the Sun:

Dear Editor:
I am 8 years old.
Some of my little friends say there is no Santa Claus.
Papa says, "If you see it in The Sun it's so." Please tell me the truth, is there a Santa Claus?
  Virginia O'Hanlon 115 West 95th Street

Virginia, your little friends are wrong. They have been affected by the skepticism of the age. They do not believe except what they see. They think that nothing can be which is not comprehensible by their little minds. All minds, Virginia, whether they are men's or children's are little. In this great universe of ours man is a mere insect, an ant, in his intellect, as compared with the boundless world about him, as measured by the intelligence capable of grasping the whole truth and knowledge,
  Yes, Virginia, there is a Santa Claus. He exists as certainly as love and generosity and devotion exist, and you know that they abound and give to your life its highest beauty and joy. Alas! how dreary would be the world it there were no Santa Claus! It would be as dreary as if there were no Virginias. There would be no childlike faith, then no poetry, no romance to make tolerable this existence. We should have no enjoyment, except in sense and sight. The eternal light with which childhood fills the world would be extinguished.
Not believe in Santa Claus! You might as well not believe in fairies! You might get your papa to hire men to watch in all the chimneys on Christmas Eve to catch Santa Claus, but even if they did not see Santa Claus coming down, what would that prove? Nobody sees Santa Claus, but that is no sign that there is no Santa Claus. The most real things in the world are those

51

*that neither children nor men can see. Did you see fairies
dancing on the lawn? Of course not, but that's no proof that
they are not there. Nobody can conceive or imagine all the
wonders there are unseen and unseeable in the world.*

*You tear apart the baby's rattle and see what makes the noise
inside, but there is a veil covering the unseen world which not
the strongest man, nor even the united strength of all the
strongest men that ever lived, could tear apart. Only faith,
fancy, beauty, love, romance, can push aside that curtain and
view and picture the supernal beauty and glory beyond. Is it
real? Ah, Virginia, in all the world there is nothing else real and
abiding. No Santa Claus! Thanks God he lives, and lives
forever. A thousand years from now, Virginia, nay 10 times
10 thousand years from now, he will continue to make glad the
heart of childhood.*

Yorkshire Pudding - A batter of flour, eggs and milk, baked in the juices of roast-
ed meats. Used by the poor for those who wanted the taste of meat,
but could not afford it.

Yule (Jul) - The Olde Norse word *jol* representing the winter solstice
celebration. It began 12 consecutive days of celebration for ending
the old year and the beginning of the new. Similar to a German word
meaning "the turning wheel" or "rising of the sun wheel" after the
winter solstice.

Yule Log - The source of light, heat, life-rebirth or the return of the sun,
"light of the world." Legends around the yule log:
- One must have twigs from last years log to ignite the Yule log of
this year.
- Those that attend the celebration would be protected for that year.
- It has the power to protect the home from evil spirits, destroy old
hatred and misunderstandings.
- The yule log traditionally must burn the 12 days for good luck.
- After the log burned out, the ashes were spread over the fields for
better crops, and the ashes were also cast into the well to purify
the water.

Yule Log Today - A chocolate cake rolled like a jelly roll.

Zahn, Matthew - Owner of the earliest known, documented American Holiday tree (December 20, 1821).

Zeus - Greek god whose battle against Kronos (time) was the Greek winter solstice seasonal celebration.

Zodiac Sign - If born on Christmas Day it is Capricorn.

Zwarte, Piet - Black Pete, from the Netherlands; a companion of St. Nicholas.

Zzzzzz - What children *should* be doing on Christmas Eve.

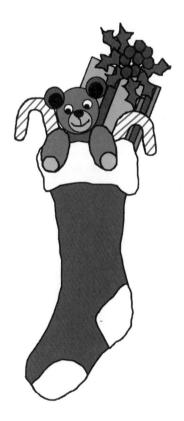

Bibliography

For further readings:

Adams, Bob. *The Everything Christmas Book.* Adams, 1994.
Auld, William. *Christmas Tidings.* Omnigraphics, 1990.
Austin, Catherine. *Christmas Past and Christmas Presents.* Sterling, 1994.
Barnett, James. *The American Christmas.* Macmillan, 1954.
Barth, Edna. *Holly, Reindeer and Colored Lights.* Seabury, 1971
Campbell, R.J. *The Story of Christmas.* Gordon, 1977.
Charlton, James. *Christmas Treasury of Yuletide.* Galahad, 1991.
Crippen, Thomas. *Christmas and Christmas Lore.* Gordon, 1976.
Miles, Clement. *Christmas Custom and Traditions: Their History and
        Significance.* Smith, 1990.
Moore, Clement. *The Night Before Christmas.* Weathervane, 1976.
Muir, Thomas. *Christmas Customs and Traditions.* Taplinger, 1977.
Remson, Al. *Where Did Christmas Come From?* Berkley, 1996.
Sansom, William. *A Book of Christmas.* McGraw Hill, 1968.
Segall, Barbara. *The Holly & The Ivy: A Celebration of Christmas.*
        Crown, 1991.
Snyder, Philip. December 25th, *The Joys of Christmas Past.*
        Dodd & Mead 1985.
Stevens, Patricia. *Merry Christmas-A History of the Holiday.* Macmillian, 1970.
Wren, Peter. *Legends, Customs and Traditions of Christmas.* Wren, 1986.
Yorgason, Maragret & Ward, Annette. *All About Christmas.* Bookcraft, 1992.

For those who scanned the Bibilography, *A Scientific Analysis of Santa's Ride*:
Within 31 hours, Santa must deliver to 91.8 million homes on Christmas Eve.
This works out to 822.6 visits per second. And Santa has 1/1000th of a second
to accomplish everything he must do. With the total trip being 75 1/2 million
miles, Santa's sleigh must move at 650 miles per second, or 3,000 times the
speed of sound. His payload (3 pounds per child) must weigh 321,300 tons.
Assuming his special reindeer can pull 3,000 pounds, Santa would need
214,200 reindeer; now the sleigh's payload is 353,430 tons. Now with 353,000
tons moving at 650 miles per second there is tremendous air resistance. The
front-leading reindeer will receive 14.3 quintillion joules of energy each second-
INSTANTANEOUS COMBUSTION. With the sonic booms created, all the reindeer will be vaporized within 4.26 thousandths of a second. Assuming a 250
pound Santa, he would be pinned to the back of his sleigh by 4,315,015 pounds
of force. Yet, every year Santa delivers! (*SPY Magazine*)

If you want additional books for your family or friends, please write to:

Do You Know What I Know?
c/o Jim Cook
Box 141184
Orlando, FL 32814
TEL/FAX 407-645-2665

Number of Books Requested   _____
  @ $7.99 each ($ total)   _____
Shipping and Handling charges (see chart*)   _____
Add $1.00 for HI, AK, PR   _____

Total Due   _____

Method of Payment: *Payable to Jim Cook*

Check or Money order
Visa (13-16 digits)
Master Card (16 digits   _____
                                           Account Number

_____   _____/_____
         Print Name   Expiration Date

_____
Authorized Signature

Shipping Address _____(Name shipped to)

                           _____(Street Address)

                           _____

                           _____(City, ST, ZIP)

                           _____Phone #
              (If we need to contact you on your order)

*Orders up to $7.99   = $3.50
  $ 8.00 to $16.00   = $4.00
  $ 16.01 to $24.00   = $5.00
  $ 24.01 and over   = $5.50